Careers in STEM
A to Z

To River,
Dream Big Dreams!
Tracy B. Jones
9/16/15

Tracy B. Jones

DORRANCE
PUBLISHING CO
EST. 1920
PITTSBURGH, PENNSYLVANIA 15238

Dorrance Publishing Co
585 Alpha Drive
Suite 103
Pittsburgh, PA 15238
Visit our website at *www.dorrancebookstore.com*

ISBN: 978-1-4809-2736-0
eISBN: 978-1-4809-2874-9

Careers in STEM
A to Z

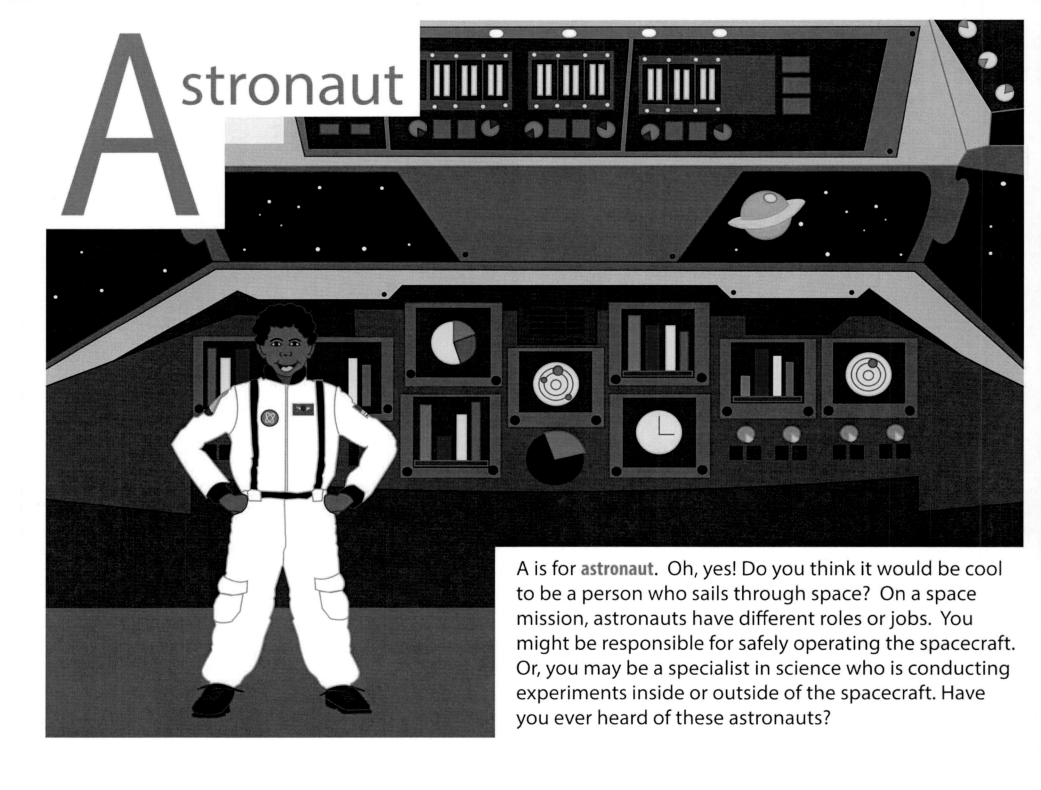

Astronaut

A is for **astronaut**. Oh, yes! Do you think it would be cool to be a person who sails through space? On a space mission, astronauts have different roles or jobs. You might be responsible for safely operating the spacecraft. Or, you may be a specialist in science who is conducting experiments inside or outside of the spacecraft. Have you ever heard of these astronauts?

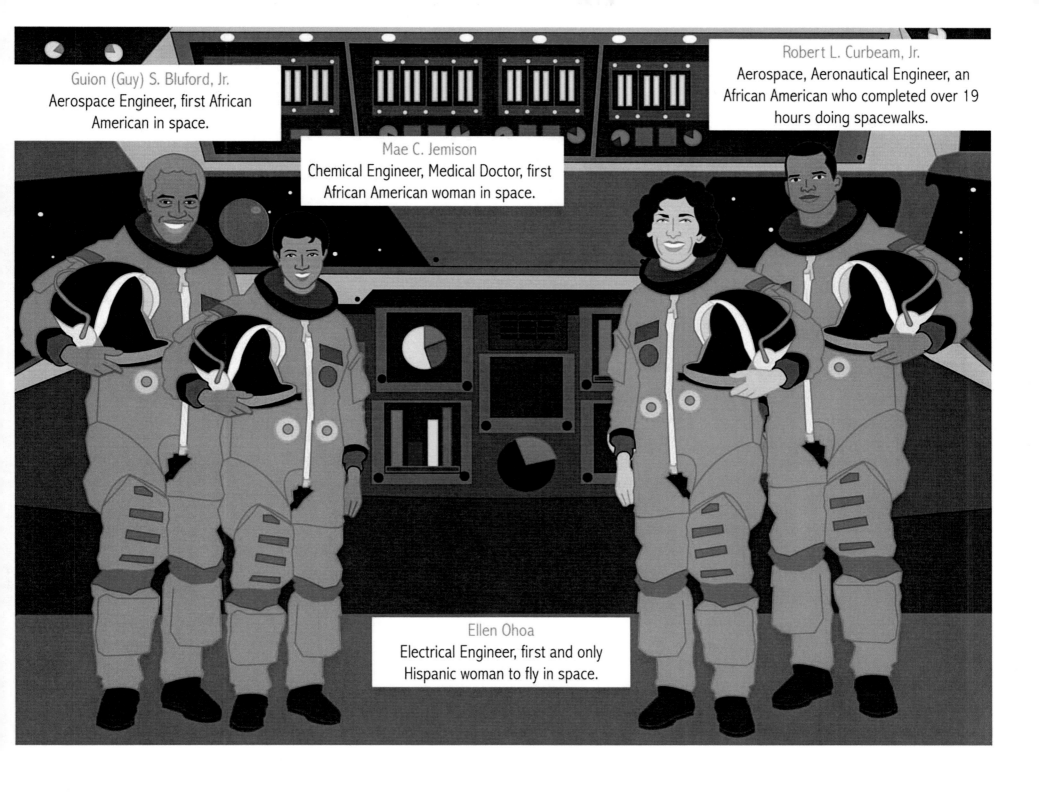

Botanist

B is for **botanist**. You may have heard of one of the great botanists in recent history named George Washington Carver. He is known as a very creative inventor because he produced over 100 uses for the peanut. How do you think he was able to do something like that? Well, he had to understand everything about the peanut. As a botanist, you study plants. Here are some reasons to study plants:

• You can develop every-day products such as glue, plastics, or lubricating oil like George Washington Carver did.

• You can help improve the way plants for medicines are grown.

Here are some of the products created by George Washington Carver. When he began to mix parts of plants with other substances, he is working as a chemist. He also helped farmers in the southern states learn how important it is to keep the soil full of nutrients. The farmers learned that they should change the crops they grow from time to time because certain crops use up too many of the nutrients needed to grow healthy plants.

Chemist

C is for chemist, mixing a little this and a little that to make something new and useful. When you are a chemist you understand why water and oil do not mix, for example. A botanist and a chemist work to create medicines that we take when we are sick. The botanist may have found an important plant in a rainforest*. A chemist like you carefully investigates the right amounts of the plant to use to make a safe medicine.

*Rainforests in places like Africa and South America are being destroyed by people at frightening speed. You might want to become a conservationist. The world needs more conservationists to take actions to save the earth's natural resources such as rainforests.

A botanist is a person who studies and understands different plants.

As a conservationist, you work towards making sure natural resources, such as rain forests, are cared for and not harmed by people.

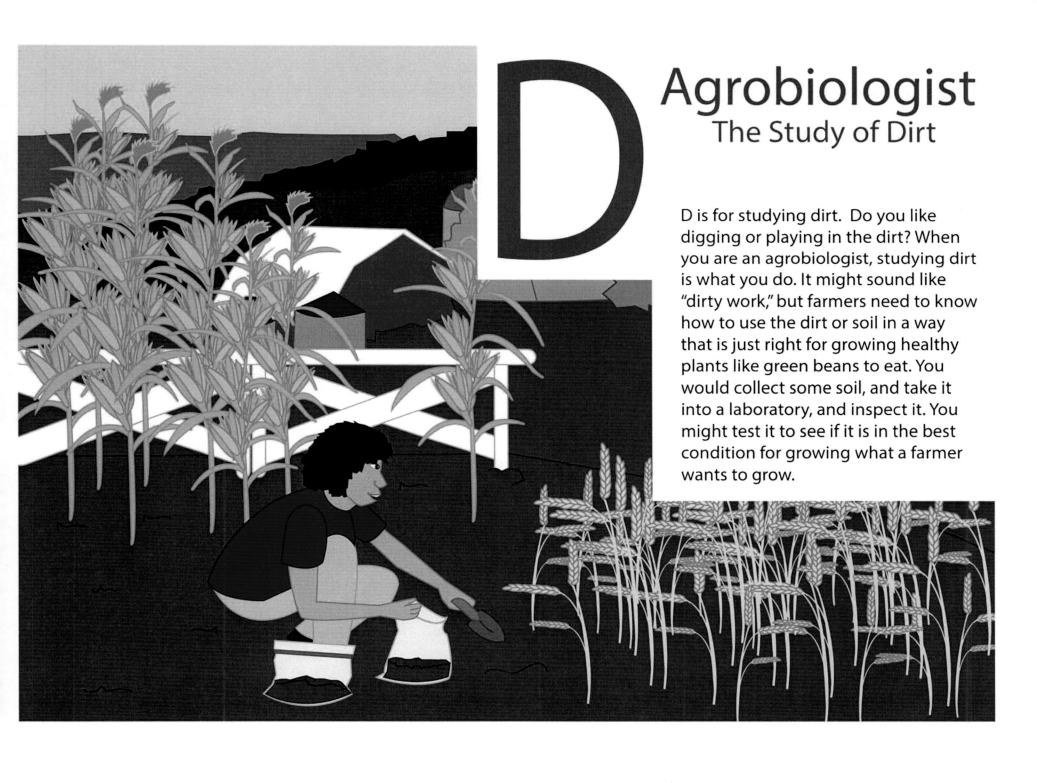

D Agrobiologist
The Study of Dirt

D is for studying dirt. Do you like digging or playing in the dirt? When you are an agrobiologist, studying dirt is what you do. It might sound like "dirty work," but farmers need to know how to use the dirt or soil in a way that is just right for growing healthy plants like green beans to eat. You would collect some soil, and take it into a laboratory, and inspect it. You might test it to see if it is in the best condition for growing what a farmer wants to grow.

Engineers

E is for engineers. All engineers solve real-world problems by combining science and special skills. Here are a few of them.

If you are an electrical engineer, you perform jobs that are connected to electricity. You might find ways to better use electrical power or computer microchips. You might be figuring out ways to keep robots, automobile engines, or cellular phones, or tablets working for longer periods of time.

When you work on the connections between software and hardware, you are a computer engineer. If you are building or improving computer programs such as games, you are working on software. When you are designing or building a computer of any size, you are working with hardware.

An aerospace engineer is like a mechanical engineer because they design and test, too. However, you would be an expert with aircrafts, spacecrafts, satellites, and missiles.

Forestry Technician

F is for forestry technician. Do you love the great outdoors? You could enjoy being a forestry technician because that is where you spend your time every day! You would care for forests, lakes, mountains, or grasslands. These are gifts of nature, and your job would be to make sure people can keep on enjoying them.

Geoscientist

G is for **geoscientist.** Are you a person who wonders about rocks, soils, and the other materials of the earth? If so, you could become a geoscientist. You would work both outside and inside a laboratory studying what is inside of the earth. Your studies would tell you about how the earth was long ago and what it might be like in the future. Who knows, you might even discover a type of rock that no one else has ever seen before!

Highway Engineer

H is for **highway engineer.** Did you ever wonder who plan the major construction projects such as bridges, airports, tunnels, or major roads and highways in your state? This is the work of civil engineers. As a highway engineer, you focus on highways and roads. You would spend most of your time in an office designing and planning. If there is a problem at a highway site, however, you go out to help solve it.

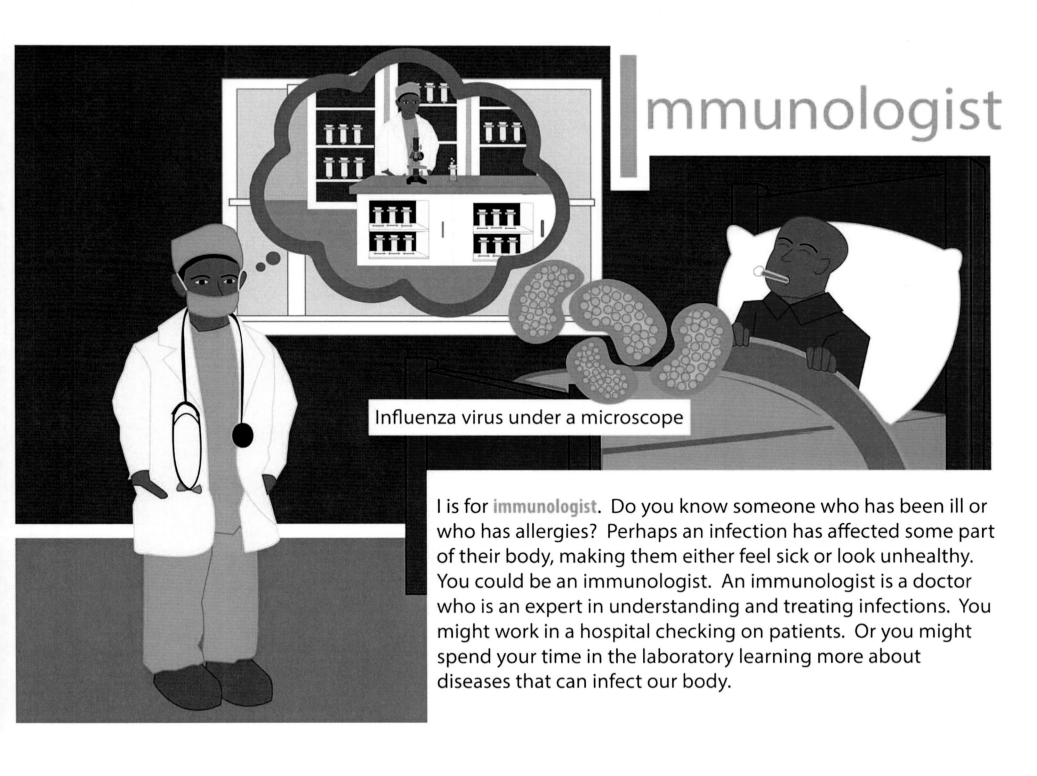

Immunologist

Influenza virus under a microscope

I is for **immunologist**. Do you know someone who has been ill or who has allergies? Perhaps an infection has affected some part of their body, making them either feel sick or look unhealthy. You could be an immunologist. An immunologist is a doctor who is an expert in understanding and treating infections. You might work in a hospital checking on patients. Or you might spend your time in the laboratory learning more about diseases that can infect our body.

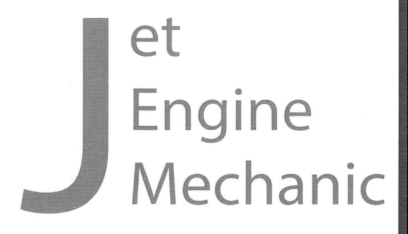

Jet Engine Mechanic

J is for **jet engine mechanic**. Have you seen jets streaking across the sky? You can be sure that a jet engine mechanic is one of the persons responsible for that jet staying up in the air and traveling at top speed. As a jet engine mechanic, you make sure a jet's engine is working the way it should. You may fix or install one of the engine's parts.

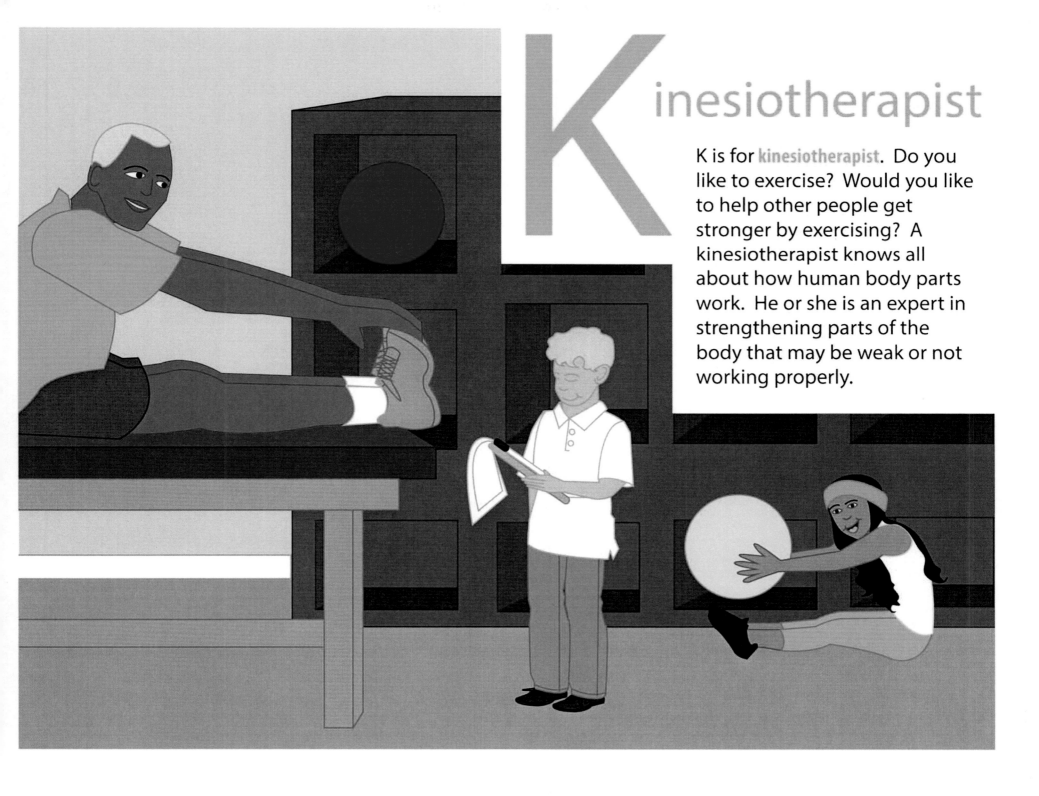

Kinesiotherapist

K is for **kinesiotherapist**. Do you like to exercise? Would you like to help other people get stronger by exercising? A kinesiotherapist knows all about how human body parts work. He or she is an expert in strengthening parts of the body that may be weak or not working properly.

Laboratory Supervisor

L is for **laboratory supervisor**. If you work in a laboratory, you might want to be the supervisor. A laboratory is a special space used for examining and investigating. If you are the supervisor, you would watch over all of the activities in the laboratory to be sure the workers are following steps carefully.

Mathematician

Math Classwork

2-2= 2x6= 10÷2=

3+9= 7x5= 60÷6=

4+8= ⬚1= 30÷3=

M is for **mathematician**. Some people are excellent with counting. They add, subtract, and estimate easily. They understand numbers and how numbers work together. Just like a sculptor molds clay into something special like a bridge, mathematicians use numbers to show how a bridge should be built so that it remains strong and able to hold whatever goes over it. Mathematicians help architects, engineers, and businesspersons with their special work.

Network Engineer

N is for **network engineer**. If you choose the career of being a network engineer, you would be making sure that computers are "talking" to each other the way people want them to "talk." When a network is working correctly, you, as the network engineer, will have made sure that the computer programs and electronic wirings are connected in a way that allows the computers to communicate information.

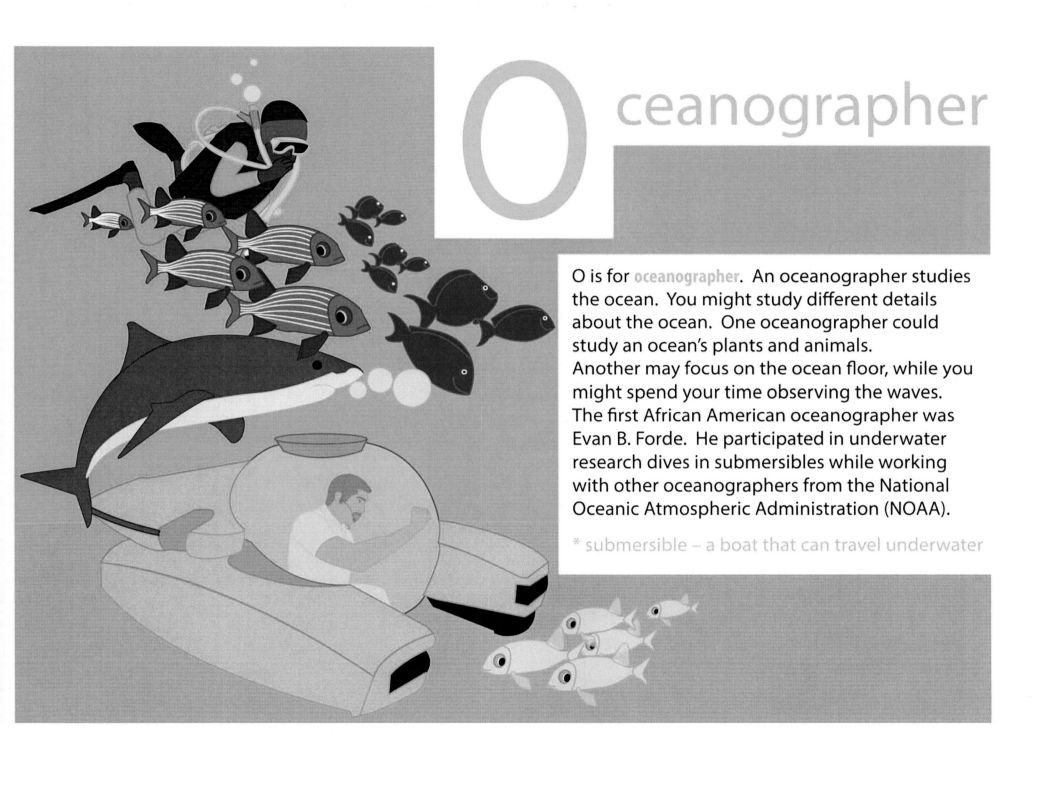

Oceanographer

O is for oceanographer. An oceanographer studies the ocean. You might study different details about the ocean. One oceanographer could study an ocean's plants and animals. Another may focus on the ocean floor, while you might spend your time observing the waves. The first African American oceanographer was Evan B. Forde. He participated in underwater research dives in submersibles while working with other oceanographers from the National Oceanic Atmospheric Administration (NOAA).

* submersible – a boat that can travel underwater

Podiatrist

P is for **podiatrist**. Do you like helping people heal if they are sick? A podiatrist is a special kind of doctor. When you are a podiatrist, you help people who have problems with their feet, ankles, or the lower section of their legs. You would tell patients what medicines to take. Or, sometimes you might have to operate on the problem area in a surgery room at a hospital or special health care center.

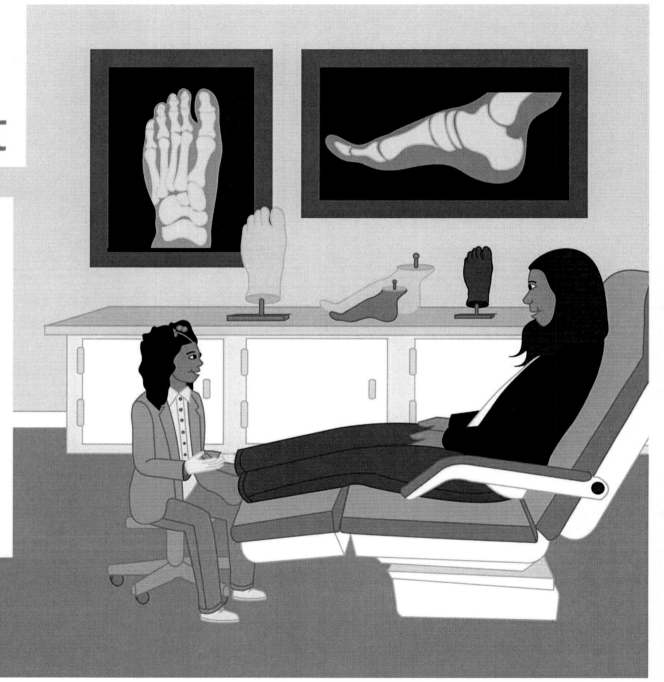

Quality Control Inspector

Q is for **quality control inspectors**. Think about your favorite milk or juice, snack, chair, or the shirt you love to wear. When you are a quality control inspector, you carefully check out products and materials made in factories to make sure they are safe and ready for use.

Range Manager

R is for **range manager**. First, you will want to know that a range is any area of land where animals may roam and feed. A range may be a wilderness owned by the United States Park Service or a state such as Maryland, or it may belong to a person. As a range manager, you must know about nature to make sure the land is being used carefully. You will check to see that the land is helpful to people, farm animals, and wildlife.

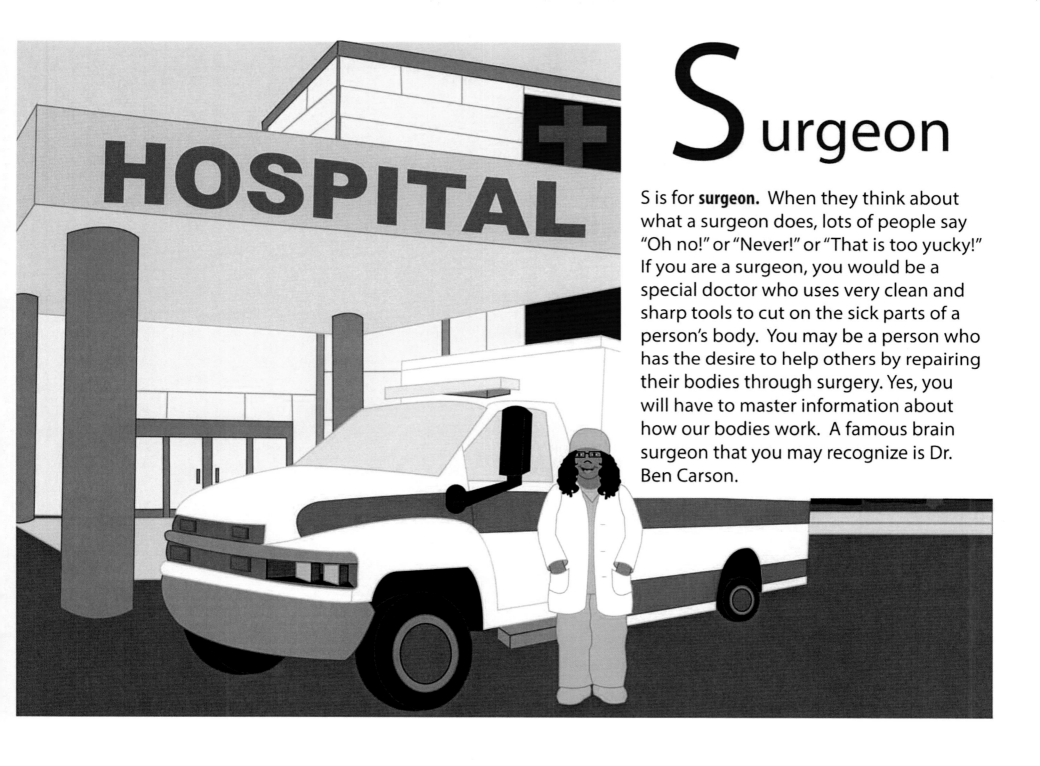

S urgeon

S is for **surgeon.** When they think about what a surgeon does, lots of people say "Oh no!" or "Never!" or "That is too yucky!" If you are a surgeon, you would be a special doctor who uses very clean and sharp tools to cut on the sick parts of a person's body. You may be a person who has the desire to help others by repairing their bodies through surgery. Yes, you will have to master information about how our bodies work. A famous brain surgeon that you may recognize is Dr. Ben Carson.

Technology Careers

T is for all kinds of **technology careers**. Do you absolutely love working on computers? Then you will want to think about technology careers. You might like designing programs that people can use for their jobs. Computer networking means that you are working on ways for computers to "talk" to each other no matter where they are. For example, your job might be to help build connections between computers in a school, an office, or one company's offices in three different countries around the world. Computer technology is the future for everyone! Don't you want to be a part of it?

Underground Study

U is for studying the **underground**. So many kids and adults enjoy walking and riding around on top of the ground. However, you might be wondering what is underground or deep down in the water in those places that we don't see every day. If you are a geoscientist, you want to know what's down there! You want to study the oil, gases, rocks, and water that are found inside of the earth. So grab a shovel and start digging!

Videogame Designer

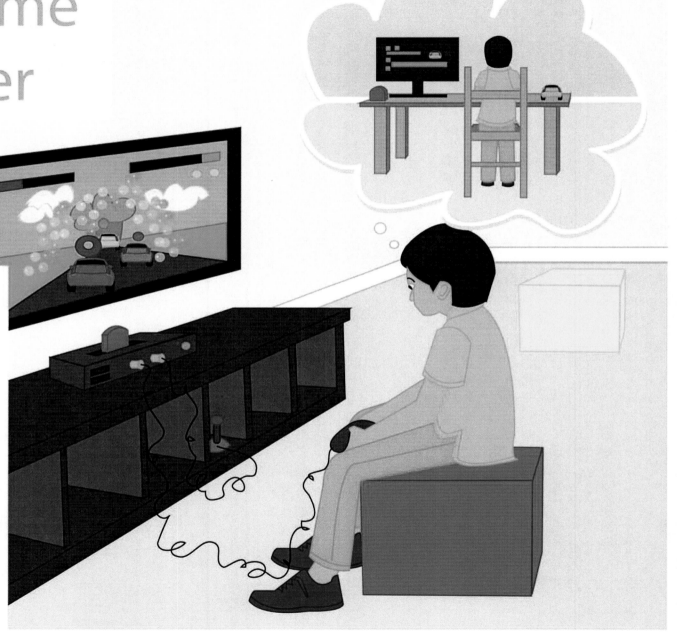

V is for videogame designer. Almost all kids love playing videogames. Now, think about whether you are creative, with tons of ideas flowing from your brain! Are you great with computers, a fantastic problem solver, and a strong communicator who enjoys working with a team? Then you are a good candidate for a career as a videogame designer. You KNOW how much kids love videogames, so go for it!

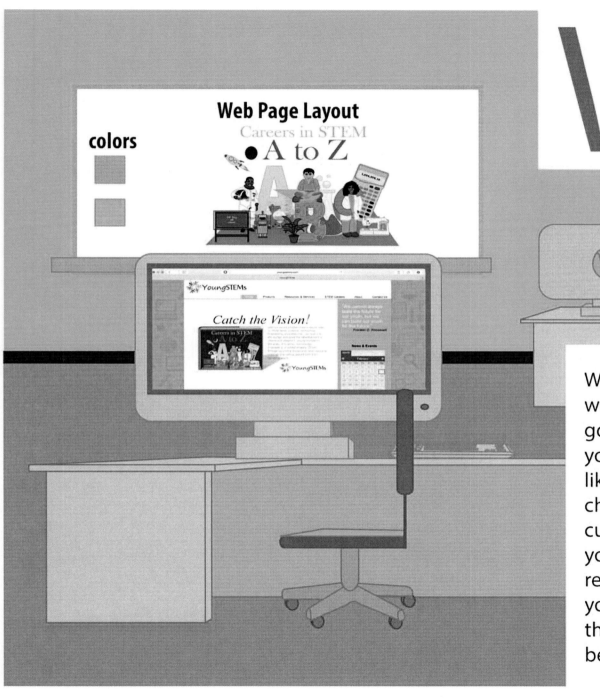

Web Designer

W is for **web designer**. What is your favorite website? Why do you like it? Why do you go back to it over and over again? When you are a web designer you know what kids like you find most interesting, fun, and challenging. Are you creative? Are you curious about graphics or art? Do you think you could use what other kids and adults really like to create or change websites? If your answer to these questions was 'yes,' then a web designer is something you can become.

X- ray Technician

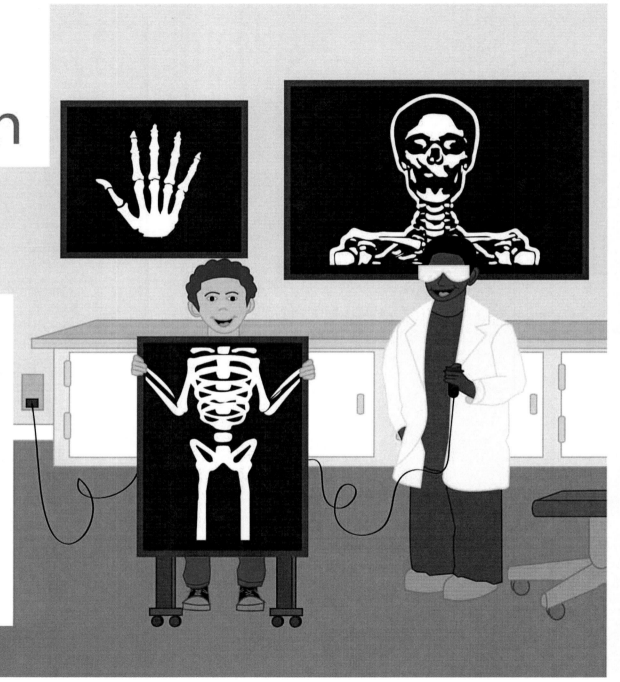

X is for **x-ray technician.** As an x-ray technician, you take pictures of the inside of people's body. You perform this job with an x-ray machine, in a room, specifically set aside for x-ray technicians and patients to use. When a doctor orders an x-ray, he or she wants to be clear in finding and treating the exact spot where there is an injury or illness. Your work as an x-ray technician is one important step in helping someone begin to heal.

Y es, that's what I want to be!

Y is for a young person yelling, *"Yes, that is what I want to be!"* Would you like designing yards or building yachts? Perhaps you can see yourself creating new yogurt flavors in a chemistry lab, learning about diseases that make young children sick, or building a robot that looks just like you. Whatever you choose, go ahead and yell it out!

Zoologist

Z is for **zoologist.** Can you imagine yourself in a damp, wet cave staring up at 200 bats clinging to the ceiling? If you absolutely love animals and care about their well-being, zoology is the career for you. Yes, like all careers, you will have to study a lot to learn information such as where animals come from, about their unique behaviors, and what diseases cause them to be ill or to die. Although an animal may never say "thank you", you can believe that caring for them is something very important to the world.